Drawing Together to Accept and Respect Differences

Written by Marge Eaton Heegaard

To be illustrated by children
to help families communicate and learn together

Fairview Press

Published by Fairview Press, 2450 Riverside Avenue, Minneapolis, Minnesota 55454. Fairview Press is a division of Fairview Health Services, a community-focused health system affiliated with the University of Minnesota and providing a complete range of services, from the prevention of illness and injury to care for the most complex medical conditions. For a free current catalog of Fairview Press titles, please call toll-free 1-800-544-8207. Or visit our Web site at www.fairviewpress.org.

ISBN-10: 1-57749-138-6
ISBN-13: 978-1-57749-138-5
First printing: November 2003

Cover by Laurie Ingram
Interior by Dorie McClelland, Spring Book Design (www.springbookdesign.com)

We gratefully acknowledge J. Thomas Viall, Shanice Buckhalton, Gena Parsons, Scott Slorby, and John Gerhardt for taking time to test this book and make helpful suggestions.

About this book

This book is designed for children ages six through twelve to illustrate with pictures they choose to draw. Younger children may need help understanding some of the words and concepts in the book, but do not offer too many suggestions. This is their book; let them make their own decisions.

I recommend that a child be given a small box of new crayons to illustrate the book. While many children enjoy drawing with markers, crayons often encourage greater self-expression. Older children may prefer to use colored pencils.

Younger children like to illustrate books because images come more naturally to them than words. Older children are more comfortable expressing themselves verbally and may use words with their illustrations.

As you and the child work through this book together, focus on ideas and expression rather than drawing ability. Do not try to protect the child from difficult feelings. As children learn to understand and express their feelings, they develop coping skills that will help them the rest of their lives. If a drawing reveals that the child has misperceived something, correct the child gently. Remember that what a child perceives to be real is as powerful to that child as any reality.

To encourage conversation, periodically invite the child to tell you more about his or her drawings. At the end of each section, you may want to tell the child something you have learned and ask the child to tell you something he or she has learned. When the book is completed, encourage the child to share his or her work with another adult for review and continued learning. Save the book as a keepsake of childhood memories.

Adults can help children accept and respect differences

Differences are what make our world rich and interesting; indeed, the very strength of our society lies in its diversity. But for children, differences can be a source of fear, discomfort, and low self-esteem. If they are to develop respect for others as well as for themselves, they need to be taught that everyone is different and special. This learning must begin in the home and continue at school and other places of adult contact.

It is important to teach children about their own race, ethnicity, religion, and culture. Ethnic foods, costumes, traditions, and rituals are particularly interesting to children. Knowledge of their ancestors and pride in their heritage can enhance self-esteem. But children must learn about other cultures as well. Schools are beginning to teach about various ethnicities, and adults can provide multicultural books and create opportunities for children to spend time with people of different backgrounds.

As children begin to establish a sense of identity, they start to compare themselves with others. Small children may suddenly wish they were taller. Tall children may wish they were smaller. It's even common for children to wish their hair, eyes, or skin were a different color.

Children will feel different because of any number of characteristics, including size, shape, gender, race, and disability. Reactions vary: a major disability may lead to few emotional problems for some children, while minor differences can create a significant disturbance for others. In some cases, mental or physical differences can lead to a sense of isolation.

In this book, children will use the art process to explore their feelings about differences. Thoughts, feelings, and inner conflicts are easier for children to express in pictures than in words. Children will improve their body image, develop a healthy sense of self, and learn coping skills for difficult situations. Moreover, art opens doors of communication between children and adults, providing an opportunity to encourage respect for differences. It strengthens problem-solving skills and fosters independence.

The activities in this book are designed to build self-confidence through creativity and self-expression. Depending on your child's special needs, you may wish to seek further information through books, support groups, and other resources.

Children who are challenged in one way are often gifted in others. Instead of feeling frustrated by their differences, children can learn skills to help them reach their full potential.

This book uses the art process to help children learn basic concepts about differences. The text is intended to help children:

To children

This is your book. You will make it different from all other books by drawing your own thoughts and feelings. You do not need any special skills to illustrate the pages. Just use lines, shapes, and colors to draw the pictures that come into your head as you read the words on each page.

Begin with the first page and do the pages in order. Ask an adult for help with words or pages you do not understand. When you have done a few pages, stop and share your work with an adult who cares about you.

Everyone feels different at different times for different reasons. I hope you will have fun doing this book and will learn to accept and respect all kinds of differences.

This is a picture of me.

(Draw yourself.)

If I could change something about myself, I would change:_____

_____.

People often wish for something different.

People come in different shapes and sizes.
(Check ✓ the words that describe you.)

_____ short	_____ just right	_____ little ears
_____ tall	_____ long legs	_____ big ears
_____ average	_____ short legs	_____ short hair
_____ big	_____ big eyes	_____ long hair
_____ thin	_____ little eyes	_____ curly hair

I am glad I am the way I am because:

_____

_____

_____

_____

Different means special. Different is O.K.!

People are colorful.

(Draw your colors. Look in a mirror or have someone tell you what colors to use.)

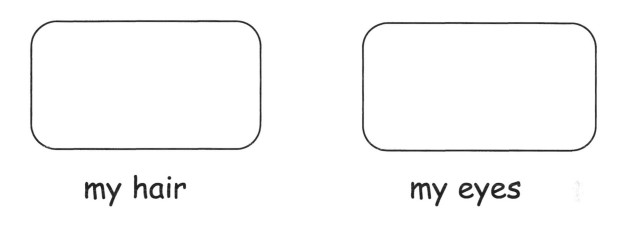

my hair   my eyes

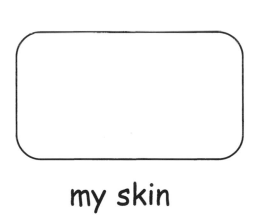

my skin

Most skin is a mix of white, yellow, pink, tan, brown, and black. No one is just white or black. We are all a mix of many colors.

I have friends I like to be with. They are all different.

(Draw a picture of your friends.)

Differences are interesting.

Sometimes I feel different from other kids.
(Draw what makes you feel different.)

A world where everyone was alike and was good at the same things would be boring.

I have many feelings.

(Draw and name some different feelings using lines, shapes, and colors.)

All feelings are O.K.

Feelings are something I feel in my body.

(Close your eyes and think of a feeling. Where in your body do you feel this feeling? Use the colors below.)

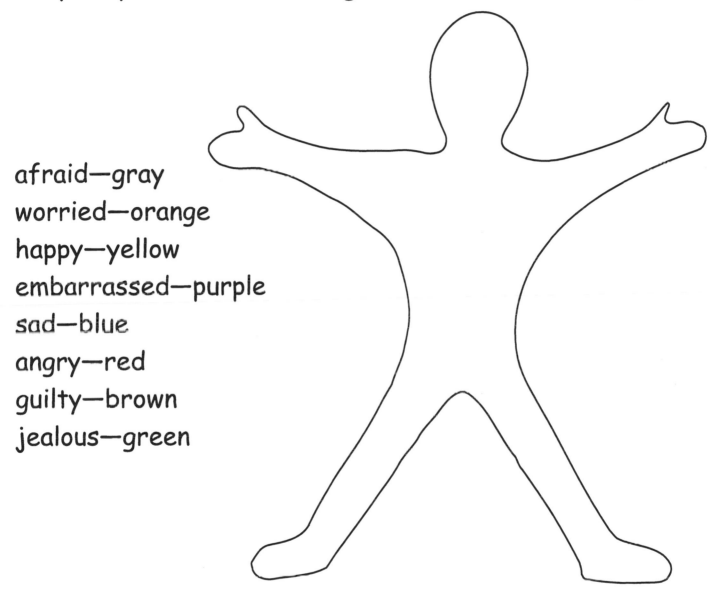

afraid—gray
worried—orange
happy—yellow
embarrassed—purple
sad—blue
angry—red
guilty—brown
jealous—green

It is important to know what you are feeling. Feelings affect your actions.

Sometimes I put on a MASK to hide my feelings.
I pretend to feel something different.

(Draw and name three feelings you try to hide.)

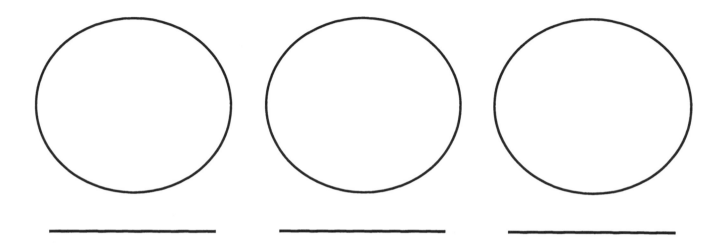

_____   _____   _____

(Draw and name the masks you use to hide these feelings.)

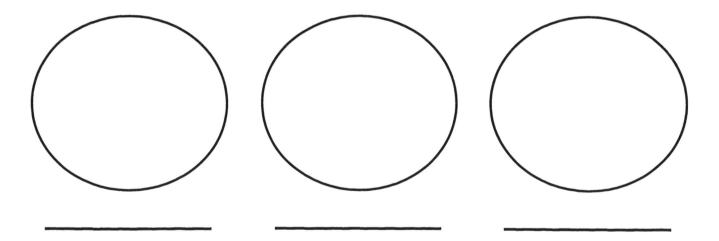

_____   _____   _____

Masks build walls between people. They make it hard
for others to get to know you.

If feelings are kept stuffed inside, they can cause aches and pains.

(Use red to color the places you get aches and pains.)

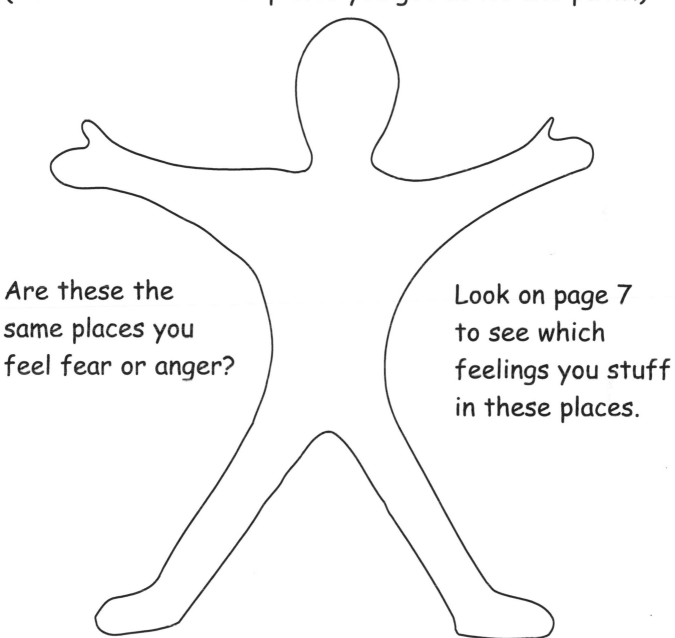

Are these the same places you feel fear or anger?

Look on page 7 to see which feelings you stuff in these places.

Everyone has feelings. You don't have to hide them.

There are times I feel left out and lonely.

(Draw a time when you felt lonely.)

When others are
gone or busy,
I have something
to comfort me.

(Draw something
that comforts you.)

You can find comfort, or you can do something for
others. Either will make you feel better.

Sometimes I feel very frightened.

(Draw a time you were afraid.)

When I am scared, I . . .

(Draw what you do.)

Everyone needs love and comfort to feel safe.

Sometimes I have scary dreams.

(Draw one of your dreams.)

Drawing your fears can make them seem smaller and help you feel better.

I feel angry when . . .
(Draw an angry time.)

It is O.K. to feel angry, but it is not O.K. to hurt people
or things.

Anger that is not expressed can turn into resentment or rage. But I can learn to let my anger out in ways that will not hurt people or things. It is O.K. to:

1. Say "I am angry because . . ."
2. Punch a pillow or throw a ball.
3. Yell into a pillow or in the shower.
4. Stomp my feet or clap my hands.
5. Write an angry letter, then tear it up.
6. Write in my journal.
7. Scribble on an old newspaper using many colors and feelings, then scrunch it into a ball and toss it against a bare wall.
8. Walk or run fast.

You are responsible for your own behavior. You can choose what to do with your anger.

Sometimes I feel sad.

(Draw a sad time.)

It is O.K. to cry to let sadness out.

Bodies are made up of bones, muscles, and nerves.

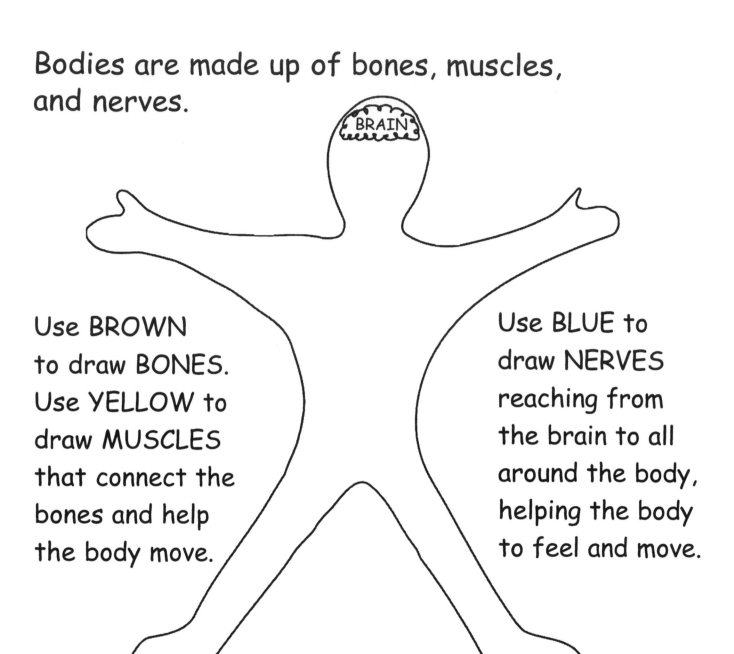

BRAIN

Use BROWN
to draw BONES.
Use YELLOW to
draw MUSCLES
that connect the
bones and help
the body move.

Use BLUE to
draw NERVES
reaching from
the brain to all
around the body,
helping the body
to feel and move.

Bodies do not all work the same way. Some people
are able to move, see, hear, and talk easily. Others
have a PHYSICAL DISABILITY and are unable to do
some things easily.

The brain stores memory, like a computer, and tells the body what to do. Not all brains are alike.

(Check ✓ the descriptions that sound like you.)

_____ Some people learn new things easily.

_____ Some people learn new things slowly.

_____ Some people remember what they learn.

_____ Some people quickly forget what they learn.

_____ Some people are good at sports.

_____ Some people are good at music or art.

_____ Some people are quiet and shy.

_____ Some people like to be noisy and silly.

_____ Some people act before thinking.

_____ Some people are afraid and worry often.

_____ Some people make friends easily.

_____ Some people have trouble getting along with others.

_____ Some people are often very sad.

_____ Some people are hyperactive.

People of all ages do things differently.

Mental or physical disabilities can make some things difficult to do. Yet many famous people have had disabilities, and they were still able to do great things.

Franklin Delano Roosevelt was unable to walk.

Helen Keller was unable to see or hear.

Abraham Lincoln suffered from depression.

Thomas Edison's teacher said he was too stupid to learn anything.

Albert Einstein did not speak until he was 4 years old.

John F. Kennedy, Walt Disney, and many others had ADHD.

Bill Cosby's 6th-grade report card said he was a "disruptive force."

Everyone has different abilities and ways of learning. Each of us must try to do our very best.

Everyone has some things that they can do well.

(Draw something easy for you to do well.)

You can help others who are having trouble.

Everyone has some things that are more difficult for them to do.

(Draw something that is hard for you to do.)

There is someone I can ask for help:

_____

You can always ask for help.

I feel helpless when . . .

(Draw a time you felt helpless.)

I feel powerful when . . .

(Draw a time you felt powerful.)

Thoughts and brain power can be stronger than muscle power!

Some children act tough to hide their fear or anger. They tease or bully others when they don't feel good about themselves.

(Draw a picture about teasing.)

Do not tease others. Try to ignore people who pick on you. Sometimes you may need help from an adult.

People live in different places. Some people live in a big city, a small town, or the country. They might live in a large house, a small house, or an apartment building.

(Draw a picture of where you live.)

People have different jobs and different needs. Home is where you live.

Any group of people who live together can be a family. Family members care about and help each other.

(Draw a picture of the people you live with having a special time together.)

There are many different kinds of families. Families have different ideas of what is important.

Sometimes people fear or dislike others who seem different. People may be treated unfairly just because of how they look, where they live, or what they do. Treating someone unfairly is called DISCRIMINATION.

(Draw a picture about discrimination.)

PREJUDICE means prejudging someone or something. Learning more can bring acceptance and caring.

A FACT is something proved to be true. An OPINION is just something I believe. Opinions can change.

(Draw someone or something you didn't think you would like but later learned you DO like.)

It is important to form opinions very carefully so you don't hurt others or miss out on good things.

My friends and I are different in some ways and alike in others. There are things we like to do together.

(Draw some of these things.)

People with the same interests often come together.

My friends and I have different opinions and feel differently about some things.

(Draw something that you and your friends argue about.)

Everyone disagrees at times. It is O.K. to talk about differences, as long as you show respect for each other.

It takes courage to be different when friends are doing something I know is wrong.

(Draw a time when you stood up to your friends.)

People like to please others, but it is more important to feel good about yourself.

The best feeling is knowing that I am me. I am special and different from everyone else!

(Draw a happy picture.)

When you are happy with yourself, you can love and help others.

Growing up is not always easy, but hard times bring special blessings. I have a special wish.

(Draw your wish.)

I will grow up and become a very special adult!